101 Quick & Easy

Cookie Recipes

Victoria Steele

Cooking 101 - Quick & Easy

COOKBOOK series

Graphics by CandO_Designs

ISBN-13: 978-1501092930

CONTENTS

101 Quick & Easy Cookie Recipes

What's better than the smell of freshly baked, homemade cookies? Eating them! So, get out a bowl and cookie sheets while you browse through this collection of delicious and simple cookies.

Whether you're in the mood for a drop cookie, refrigerator cookie, bar cookie or no-bake cookie, you're sure to find the perfect treat for after school snacks, late night munching or gifts for family and friends.

With over 100 cookie recipes, you'll never be short on ideas for your next cookie baking adventure. These recipes are all made with the ingredients you probably already have on hand, and are simple and fast from start to finish. You and the family will be enjoying a sweet treat in no time, and the simple recipes make cleanup a snap.

Make traditional favorites like Peanut Butter Cookies or Chocolate Chip cookies, or try something new like Cashew Cookies or Coconut Baboon Cookies. You'll also find simple recipes your kids can make themselves, like no-bake Chow Mein Cookies and Almond Bark Cookies. These are great for Saturday night sleep-overs and slumber parties.

Bar cookies are perfect for pot luck get-togethers and are sure to get rave reviews from all the guests. You'll also find frosted cookies and cut-out cookies that are fun to decorate for any holiday or event.

So, take out your apron, put on your favorite music, pick out your favorite recipe and start baking a sweet treat the entire family will enjoy.

Fruit Cookies
Satin Drop Cookies

Drop cookies are the easiest to make. Just mix the dough, drop and bake!

1/4 cup butter or margarine, softened
3/4 cup brown sugar, packed
1/2 cup sour cream
1 egg
1 teaspoon vanilla
1 1/4 cups all-purpose flour
1/2 teaspoon baking soda
1/4 teaspoon baking powder
1/2 lb. dates, chopped
1/2 cup nuts, chopped
1/2 cup maraschino cherries, cut in large pieces

Mix butter or margarine, brown sugar, sour cream, egg and vanilla thoroughly. Blend in flour, baking soda and baking powder. Stir in dates, nuts and cherries. Drop by teaspoonful on lightly greased cookie sheet. Bake in preheated oven at 400 degrees F for 10 minutes.

Yield: 4 dozen.

Moist Raisin Cookies

You can probably find most of the ingredients for these simple cookies in your kitchen pantry.

1 cup raisins
1 cup butter or margarine, softened
1 cup granulated sugar
2 eggs
1 teaspoon vanilla
5 tablespoons raisin juice
1 teaspoon baking soda
1 teaspoon cinnamon
2 cups quick oats
2 cups all-purpose flour
1/2 teaspoon salt

Simmer raisins covered with water until plump; drain except for 5 tablespoons raisin juice.

Beat together butter or margarine, granulated sugar, eggs and vanilla. Add raisin juice with baking soda, cinnamon, oats, flour, and salt. Stir in raisins. Drop by teaspoonfuls on cookie sheet. Bake in preheated oven at 350 degrees F for 12 minutes.

Yield: 2 dozen cookies.

Apple Cookies with Vanilla Glaze

These hearty apple cookies are chock-full of apples, raisins and nuts.

1/2 cup margarine, softened
1 1/3 cups brown sugar, packed
1 egg
1/4 cup milk
2 cups all-purpose flour
1 teaspoon baking soda
1 teaspoon nutmeg
1 teaspoon cinnamon
1/2 teaspoon cloves
1 cup apples, diced
1 cup raisins
1 cup nuts, chopped

Cream together margarine and brown sugar. Add egg and milk. Combine flour, baking soda, nutmeg, cinnamon and cloves. Stir into creamed mixture. Add apples, raisins and nuts. Bake in preheated oven at 400 degrees F for 8 to 10 minutes. Drizzle glaze over warm cookies.

Glaze:
1 1/2 cups confectioners' sugar
1 tablespoon butter or margarine, melted
1 teaspoon vanilla
1/8 teaspoon salt
2 to 4 tablespoons milk
Mix all glaze ingredients together.

Yield: 4 dozen.

Candied Fruit Cookies

Dried fruit and lots of nuts make these fruit cookies a perfect winter treat.

1/2 cup all-purpose flour
1/2 teaspoon salt
2 egg whites
1/2 cup granulated sugar
1 tablespoon vanilla
1 cup pecans, chopped
1 cup walnuts, chopped
1 cup Brazil nuts, chopped
3/4 lb. red & green candied cherries, chopped
3/4 lb. candied pineapple, chopped

Mix flour and salt together. Dredge pecans, walnuts, Brazil nuts and fruit in flour mixture to coat all sides. Beat egg whites until stiff then slowly add granulated sugar. Add vanilla. Fold fruit and nut mixture into beaten egg white mixture. Drop cookies by tablespoonfuls on greased cookie sheet. Bake in preheated oven at 350 degrees F for 12 to 15 minutes. Remove from cookie sheet immediately.

Yield: 4 dozen.

Linzer Cookies

These beautiful cookies are little more labor intensive than some of the other recipes, but it is well worth the effort.

1 cup butter, softened
1/2 cup granulated sugar
1 teaspoon vanilla
2 cups all-purpose flour
1/4 teaspoon salt
Apricot or strawberry preserves
Confectioners' sugar

Cream butter, granulated sugar and vanilla until light and foamy. Combine flour and salt; add to sugar mixture and stir to make a smooth dough. Roll out the dough 1/4 " thick and cut into 3" rounds with cookie cutter. Using a small cookie cutter, cut the centers out of just half of the rounds.

Bake rings and rounds in preheated oven at 375 degrees F for 10 minutes or until they are golden on the edges. When cool, spread rounds with drained apricot or strawberry preserves and place a ring on each to make a cookie sandwich. Put a little more jam in the hole. Dust with confectioners' sugar.

Yield: 1 dozen.

Banana Spice Cookies

These banana spice cookies are quick and easy to make and with ingredients like cinnamon and cloves, they are a great addition to a winter breakfast.

1/2 cup margarine, softened
1 cup brown sugar, packed
2 eggs
1 cup bananas, mashed
2 cups all-purpose flour
2 teaspoons baking powder
1/4 teaspoon cinnamon
1/4 teaspoon cloves
1/4 teaspoon salt
1/4 teaspoon baking soda
1/2 cup nuts, chopped

Combine margarine, brown sugar and eggs. Stir in bananas; mix well. Combine flour, baking powder, cinnamon, cloves, salt and baking soda; add to sugar mixture. Add nuts. Chill in refrigerator about 1 hour. Drop by rounded teaspoonfuls of dough on lightly greased cookie sheets. Bake in preheated oven at 375 degrees F to 10 minutes.

Yield: 3 to 4 dozen cookies.

Pumpkin Nut Cookies

These cookies can be frosted with your favorite cream cheese frosting.

1 cup brown sugar, packed
1 cup pumpkin, canned or cooked
1/4 cup vegetable oil
1/4 cup margarine or butter, softened
1 teaspoon vanilla
2 cups all-purpose flour
1 teaspoon baking soda
1 teaspoon baking powder
1/2 teaspoon cinnamon
1/2 teaspoon nutmeg
1/2 teaspoon salt
1/4 teaspoon ginger
1 cup dates, chopped
1/2 cup nuts, chopped

In a large bowl, beat brown sugar, pumpkin, vegetable oil, margarine or butter and vanilla together. In a separate bowl, combine flour, baking soda, baking powder, cinnamon, nutmeg, salt and ginger. Add to sugar mixture; stir until smooth. Stir in dates and nuts. Drop by teaspoonfuls on greased cookie sheets. Bake in preheated oven at 350 degrees F for 12 to 15 minutes.

Yield: 3 to 4 dozen.

Drop Date Cookies

Enjoy the sweet taste of dates in these delectable soft cookies.

1 cup margarine or butter, softened
1 1/2 cups granulated sugar
1 teaspoon baking soda
3 eggs
2 tablespoons corn syrup
3 cups all-purpose flour
1 teaspoon cinnamon
1/2 teaspoon cloves
1/2 teaspoon nutmeg
1 lb. dates, chopped

Cream margarine or butter and granulated sugar. Dissolve baking soda in 2 tablespoons of boiling water and add to sugar mixture. Add eggs and corn syrup; mix well.

In another bowl, mix flour, cinnamon, cloves and nutmeg. Add to sugar mixture. Add dates and mix well. Drop cookie dough on greased and floured cookie sheets. Bake in preheated oven at 350 degrees F until brown, about 10 to 12 minutes.

Yield: 4 dozen cookies.

Orange Drop Cookies

The orange-lemon touch adds a special taste to ordinary cookies.

2/3 cup butter or margarine, softened
3/4 cup granulated sugar
1 egg
1/2 cup orange juice
2 tablespoons grated orange rind, optional
2 cups all-purpose flour
1/2 teaspoon salt
1/2 teaspoon baking powder
1/2 teaspoon baking soda

Mix butter or margarine and granulated sugar; add egg and mix thoroughly. Stir in orange juice and rind. Combine flour, salt, baking powder and baking soda; add to sugar mixture and mix well. Drop by rounded teaspoonful of dough 2" apart on ungreased cookie sheet. Bake in preheated oven at 375 degrees F for 8 to 10 minutes.

Orange Frosting:

2 1/2 tablespoons butter, softened
1 1/2 cups confectioners' sugar
1 1/2 tablespoons orange juice
2 teaspoons grated orange rind, optional

Combine all ingredients and frost cooled cookies.

Yield: 4 dozen.

Raisin Chip Cookies

Enjoy a cold glass of milk and a delicious raisin chip cookie for a treat that can't be beat.

1/2 cup butter or margarine, softened
1 cup granulated sugar
1 cup brown sugar, packed
1/2 cup creamy peanut butter
2 eggs
1 teaspoon vanilla extract
1 3/4 cups all-purpose flour
1 teaspoon baking soda
1/2 teaspoon salt
1/4 cup milk
2 1/2 cups old-fashioned rolled oats
1/2 cup raisins
1/2 cup chocolate chips

Cream butter, granulated sugar and brown sugar. Add peanut butter, eggs and vanilla; mix well. In a separate bowl, mix flour, baking soda and salt; add to sugar mixture, alternating with milk. Stir in oats, raisins and chocolate chips. Drop by rounded tablespoonfuls of dough on ungreased cookie sheets. Bake in preheated oven at 350 degrees F for 12 to 15 minutes.

Yield: 5 dozen.

Peanut Butter Cookies

Peanut Butter Jumbos

These extra-large cookies are perfect for grabbing on the way out the door.

1 1/2 cups brown sugar, packed
1 1/2 cups granulated sugar
1 1/2 cups peanut butter
1 1/2 cups butter, softened
3 eggs
3 cups all-purpose flour
1 1/2 teaspoons baking soda
2 cups peanut butter chips

In a large mixing bowl, combine brown sugar, granulated sugar, peanut butter and butter; beat until fluffy. Beat in eggs. Combine flour and baking soda. Stir into egg mixture. Stir in the peanut butter chips. Drop the cookie dough by a level 1/4 measuring cup 3-inches apart on greased cookie sheets. Bake in preheated oven at 350 degrees F for about 15 minutes or until golden. Cool cookies on cookie sheet for 3 minutes. Remove cookies to wire rack, cool completely.

Yield: 32 cookies.

Peanut Butter Sandwich Cookies

A rich, addictive cookie for lovers of peanut butter and jelly.

1/2 cup margarine or butter, softened
1/2 cup granulated sugar
1/2 cup brown sugar, packed
1 egg
1/2 cup peanut butter
1 1/4 cups all-purpose flour
3/4 teaspoon baking soda
1/2 teaspoon baking powder
1/4 teaspoon salt
Jelly or jam

Mix thoroughly margarine or butter, granulated sugar, brown sugar, egg and peanut butter. Combine flour, baking soda, baking powder and salt. Stir into sugar mixture. Place dough in an airtight container and refrigerate for at least an hour.

Shape dough into 3/4-inch balls. Place about 2 inches apart on lightly greased cookie sheets. Bake in preheated oven at 375 F about 10 minutes or until set but not hard. When cool, put cookies together in pairs with jelly filling.

Yield: 4 1/2 dozen cookies.

Peanut Butter Chip Cookies

Peanut butter fans will love this soft, buttery, rich cookie.

2 1/4 cups granulated sugar
1 1/2 cups butter, softened
1 tablespoon vanilla extract
3 eggs
3 cups all-purpose flour
1 cup unsweetened cocoa powder
3/4 teaspoon salt
1 teaspoon baking soda
3 cups peanut butter chips

Cream the granulated sugar and butter; whip until fluffy. Add vanilla and eggs. In a separate bowl, mix flour, cocoa powder, salt and baking soda. Add to sugar mixture. Gently stir in peanut butter chips.

Drop by tablespoonfuls on greased cookie sheets and bake in preheated oven at 350 degrees F for 11 minutes.

Yield: 3 dozen cookies.

Peanut Butter Cookies with Chocolate Frosting

This peanut butter cookie is a crispy cookie with a touch of chocolate.

1/2 cup margarine, softened
1 cup granulated sugar
1/2 cup peanut butter
1 egg
1 teaspoon vanilla
1 1/2 cups all-purpose flour
1/2 teaspoon baking soda
1/2 teaspoon salt
2 tablespoons milk
1 6-oz. pkg. semi-sweet chocolate chips

Cream margarine, granulated sugar and peanut butter. Add egg and vanilla. In a separate bowl, combine flour, baking soda and salt; add flour mixture to sugar mixture; add milk and mix well.

On a lightly floured surface, roll dough 1/4 inch thick. Cut with a 2" cookie cutter. Place cookies on an ungreased cookie sheet and bake in preheated oven at 350 degrees F for 10 minutes. Melt chocolate chips in microwave on 50% power until melted, stirring occasionally. Spread chocolate on cooled cookies.

Yield: 3 dozen cookies.

Classic Peanut Butter Cookies

An old-fashioned, classic favorite cookie.

1 cup granulated sugar
1 cup margarine, softened
1 cup brown sugar, packed
2 eggs, beaten
3/4 cup peanut butter
2 1/2 cups all-purpose flour
1 teaspoon baking soda
1 teaspoon salt
1 teaspoon vanilla

Cream together granulated sugar, margarine and brown sugar. Add eggs and peanut butter. Mix baking soda and salt with flour and add to sugar mixture. Add vanilla. Drop by teaspoonfuls on greased cookie sheets. Press flat with fork dipped in sugar. Bake in preheated oven for 12 to 15 minutes at 350 degrees F.

Variation:
Add 1 cup chopped peanuts to the dough before baking.

Yield: 4 dozen cookies.

Sugar Cookies
Best Sugar Cookies

These easy cookies are crisp and buttery. Bake for 10 minutes for a crunchy cookie, or 8 minutes for a soft cookie.

3 cups all-purpose flour
1 teaspoon salt
1/2 teaspoon baking soda
2/3 cup butter or margarine, softened
1 1/2 cups granulated sugar
2 eggs
2 teaspoons vanilla extract

Cream butter or margarine and granulated sugar; add eggs and vanilla. In a separate bowl, mix together flour, salt and baking soda. Combine with sugar mixture.

Chill thoroughly in refrigerator for 1 to 4 hours; then roll out on floured surface. Cut in shapes with cookie cutters and sprinkle with granulated sugar or bake plain and decorate with colored icing. Bake on a parchment-lined cookie sheet in preheated oven at 350 degrees F for 10 minutes or less.

Yield: 4 dozen cookies.

Brown Sugar Cookies

This recipe could be varied by adding M&M's or chocolate chips.

1 cup butter, softened
3/4 cup brown sugar, firmly packed
1 egg yolk
2 cups all-purpose flour
84 pecan halves

Cream the butter; gradually add brown sugar. Blend in the egg yolk. Add the flour in fourths, mixing well after each addition. Shape dough into 1-inch balls. Place on cookie sheets about 2" apart.

Using a fork, flatten cookies with crisscross marks. Press a pecan half on the top of each cookie. Bake in preheated oven at 375 degrees F for 8 to 10 minutes.

Yield: 7 dozen cookies.

Angel Cookies

This is a simple and delicious crispy sugar cookie.

1/2 cup butter or margarine, softened
1/2 cup brown sugar, packed
1/2 cup granulated sugar
1/2 cup vegetable oil
1 teaspoon vanilla
1 egg
2 cups all-purpose flour
1 teaspoon baking soda
1 teaspoon salt
1 teaspoon cream of tartar
1/2 cup walnuts, chopped

Cream butter or margarine, brown sugar and granulated sugar together. Add vegetable oil, vanilla and egg. In a separate bowl, mix flour, baking soda, salt and cream of tartar. Combine flour mixture with sugar mixture. Fold in walnuts.

Roll dough into 1-inch balls and dip the top half in cold water. Then dip in granulated sugar. Place on greased or parchment-lined cookie sheet with the sugar side up. Bake in preheated oven at 400 degrees F for 8 to 10 minutes.

Yield: 2 dozen cookies.

Dutch Sugar Cookies

This is a soft sugar cookie, perfect for using with cookie cutters.

1 cup granulated sugar
1/2 cup dairy sour cream
1/2 cup butter, softened
1 egg, beaten
1 1/2 teaspoons vanilla
1 teaspoon baking soda
1/2 teaspoon salt
3 1/4 cups all-purpose flour

With an electric mixer, cream granulated sugar, sour cream and butter together. Add beaten egg and vanilla; beat for one minute. Combine flour with baking soda and salt. Add half the dry ingredients to batter and beat for one minute.

Stir in the rest of the dry ingredients. Roll dough out on floured surface, cut with cookie cutter and sprinkle with granulated sugar. Bake in preheated oven at 400 degrees F for 8 to 10 minutes.

Yield: 5 dozen cookies.

No Roll Sugar Cookies

Need a simple, quick homemade cookie recipe? Here ya go...

1 cup butter, softened
2 cups granulated sugar
1 teaspoon vanilla
2 eggs
3 cups all-purpose flour
2 teaspoons cream of tartar
2 teaspoons baking soda
1 teaspoon salt

Cream butter and granulated sugar together; add vanilla and eggs and mix well. Combine flour with cream of tartar, baking soda and salt; add to sugar mixture. Roll into balls and roll in granulated sugar. Press with fork or glass. Bake in preheated oven at 350 degrees F for 8 to 10 minutes or until lightly brown.

Yield: 2 dozen cookies.

Frosted Soft Sugar Cookies

These cookies are soft and excellent. Great with frosting too!

3 cups all-purpose flour
1/2 teaspoon cream of tartar
1 cup margarine or butter, softened
1 teaspoon baking soda
1 cup granulated sugar
2 eggs, beaten
1 teaspoon vanilla

Mix flour, cream of tartar, margarine or butter and baking soda with fork until well blended and crumbly. Mix granulated sugar and eggs in small bowl until all sugar is dissolved and then mix with the butter mixture in large bowl. The dough will be thick. Add vanilla and mix well.

Chill the dough in refrigerator for 1 hour. Flour the counter well and roll dough out to no less than 1/4-inch thick. (You can't over-flour the dough.) Cut out cookie shapes and bake in preheated oven at 425 degrees F for only 4 minutes. When cool, frost.

Frosting:
2 1/2 cups confectioners' sugar
3 tablespoons milk
6 tablespoons butter, softened
1/2 teaspoon vanilla
Mix all ingredients together. If too thick, add a couple of drops of milk at a time to thin. Add food coloring, if desired.

Yield: 4 dozen cookies.

Chocolate Chip Cookies
Choco-Chip Cookies

This basic chocolate chip recipe is sure to become one of your favorites.

2 1/2 cups all-purpose flour
1/4 teaspoon salt
1 teaspoon baking soda
1 cup butter, melted
1 cup brown sugar, packed
1/2 cup granulated sugar
2 teaspoons vanilla
2 eggs
2 cups chocolate chips

In a large bowl, mix together flour, salt and baking soda; set aside. In a separate bowl, with an electric mixer at medium speed, beat butter, brown sugar and granulated sugar until combined well. Mix in vanilla and eggs. Add the flour mixture and beat until well mixed. Mix in chocolate chips. Drop by heaping tablespoonfuls on cookie sheets. Bake in preheated oven at 300 degrees F for 18 to 20 minutes.

Yield: 4 dozen cookies.

Chocolate-Butterscotch Chip Oatmeal Cookies

A chewy oatmeal cookie with 2 kinds of chips. Nuts are optional.

2 cups all-purpose flour
1 teaspoon baking soda
1/2 teaspoon salt
1/2 teaspoon baking powder
1/2 cup butter or margarine, softened
1/2 cup vegetable oil
1 cup brown sugar, packed
1 cup granulated sugar
2 eggs
2 cups quick oats
1 cup chocolate chips
1 cup butterscotch chips
1 teaspoon vanilla

Mix flour, baking soda, salt and baking powder. In a separate bowl, cream butter or margarine, vegetable oil, brown sugar and granulated sugar. Add eggs and beat. Add flour mixture and mix well. Stir in oats, chocolate chips, butterscotch chips and vanilla. Bake in preheated oven at 350 degrees F for 12 to 15 minutes.

Yield: 3 1/2 to 4 dozen cookies.

Classic Chocolate Chip Cookies

This is a perfect chocolate chip cookie. Chewy on the inside and crisp on the outside.

2 cups butter, softened
4 eggs
2 cups granulated sugar
2 cups brown sugar, packed
2 teaspoons vanilla
4 cups all-purpose flour
1 teaspoon salt
2 teaspoons baking soda
5 cups quick oats
1-8 oz. chocolate candy bar (plain or with almonds)
1-12 oz. package semi-sweet chocolate chips
1-12 oz. package milk chocolate chips
Any amount of chopped nuts (optional)

In a large bowl, cream butter, eggs, granulated sugar, brown sugar and vanilla. Put the 5 cups of quick oats in a blender and blend until the consistency is very fine. In another bowl, mix together flour, salt, baking soda and oats. Add to creamed mixture and mix just until well blended. Break the candy bar into small pieces. Stir in candy bar, chocolate chips and nuts.

Use a small ice cream scoop to shape cookies, or roll into big balls (they will flatten during baking). Bake in preheated oven at 325 degrees F for 7 to 10 minutes.

Yield: 8 dozen cookies.

Chocolate Honey Cookies

Soft, delicious and easy to make cookies!

1/2 cup butter, softened
1/2 cup honey
1/2 teaspoon vanilla
1 egg
1 1/2 cups all-purpose flour
1/2 teaspoon baking soda
1/2 teaspoon salt
1/4 teaspoon baking powder
1 cup chocolate chips
1/2 cups nuts, chopped

In a large bowl, cream butter and honey until light and fluffy. Add vanilla and egg. In another bowl, mix together flour, baking soda, salt and baking powder; add to first mixture. Stir in chocolate chips and nuts. On greased cookie sheets, drop dough by teaspoonful. Bake in preheated oven at 350 degrees F for 10 to 12 minutes.

Yield: 1 1/2 dozen cookies.

Cherry Chip Cookies

This light and crisp cookie uses cherry chips instead of chocolate chips.

1 cup butter or margarine, softened
1/2 cup granulated sugar
1 teaspoon almond extract
1 egg yolk
2 1/4 cups all-purpose flour
1/8 teaspoon salt
1-10 oz. package cherry chips
3/4 cup cornflakes, crushed

In a large bowl, cream butter or margarine and granulated sugar until light and fluffy. Mix in almond extract and egg yolk. Mix flour and salt together. Add flour to sugar mixture; mix until smooth. Stir in cherry chips and cornflakes.

Roll into 1-inch balls and place on ungreased cookie sheets. Press with fork lengthwise and crosswise and sprinkle with granulated sugar, if desired. Bake in preheated oven at 375 degrees F for 12 to 15 minutes.

Yield: 6 dozen cookies.

Christmas Cookies
Holiday Cookies

This super easy recipe is decorated for the holidays with red and green cherries.

1 cup butter, softened
1 cup confectioners' sugar
1 egg
1 teaspoon vanilla
2 1/2 cups all-purpose flour
1/2 cup red cherries, chopped
1/2 cup green cherries, chopped
1 cup pecans, chopped

Cream butter and confectioners' sugar; add egg and vanilla then flour. Stir in cherries and pecans. Form into long rolls. Refrigerate 4 hours or overnight, until firm. Slice the rolls into 1/4" slices and bake on cookie sheets in preheated oven at 350 degrees F for 10 to 12 minutes.

Yield: 4 dozen cookies.

Dutch Santa Claus Cookies

Not just for Santa, these delicious cookies are good any time of the year.

2 cups brown sugar, packed
1 1/2 cups butter, softened
1 egg, beaten
3 1/2 cups all-purpose flour
1 teaspoon cinnamon
1 teaspoon baking powder
1/2 teaspoon cloves
1/2 teaspoon nutmeg
1/2 teaspoon salt

Cream brown sugar and butter; add egg. In a separate bowl, mix flour, cinnamon, baking powder, cloves, nutmeg and salt. Add to sugar mixture. This makes a very stiff dough. Form into long rolls. Refrigerate 4 hours or overnight, until firm. Slice the rolls into 1/4" slices and bake in preheated oven at 350 degrees F for 10 to 12 minutes.

Yield: 4 dozen cookies.

Fruitcake Cookies

Even non-fruitcake lovers will devour these tasty cookies.

1 cup butter or margarine, softened
1 1/2 cups brown sugar, packed
2 eggs
1 teaspoon vanilla
2 1/2 cups all-purpose flour
1 teaspoon baking soda
1 teaspoon cinnamon
1/2 teaspoon salt
1 lb. dates, chopped
1 cup walnuts, chopped

Cream butter or margarine and brown sugar. Add eggs and vanilla. Beat well. Mix flour with baking soda, cinnamon and salt; add to creamed mixture. Mix the dates and walnuts together and add to mixture. Mix well. Drop by teaspoonfuls on greased cookie sheets. Bake in preheated oven at 350 degrees F for 10 minutes.

Yield: 4 dozen cookies.

Pumpkin Spiced Ice Cookies

This is a wonderful harvest cookie with spices that proclaim the holidays are coming.

1 cup granulated sugar
1 cup margarine, softened
1 (16 oz.) can solid-pack pumpkin
2 eggs
1 teaspoon vanilla
2 1/4 cups all-purpose flour
1/2 teaspoon baking soda
1 teaspoon baking powder
1/2 teaspoon salt
1 1/2 teaspoons pumpkin pie spice
1 cup walnuts, chopped
1 (12 oz.) package semi-sweet chocolate chips

Glaze:

1 cup confectioners' sugar
1 tablespoon milk
1/2 teaspoon vanilla

In a large bowl, beat granulated sugar and margarine until creamy. Add pumpkin, eggs and vanilla. In a separate bowl, combine flour, baking soda, baking powder, salt and pumpkin pie spice. Add to sugar mixture; mix well.

Stir in nuts and chocolate chips. Drop cookies by teaspoonfuls on greased cookie sheets. Bake in preheated oven at 350 degrees F for 13 to 15 minutes, or until edges are lightly browned. Let stand for 5 minutes. Remove from cookie sheet and cool. Combine glaze ingredients and spread on baked cookies.

Yield: 5 1/2 dozen.

Poinsettia Sandwich Cookies

These almond topped treats are a nice festive change from everyday cookies.

2 cups all-purpose flour
1 1/3 cups almonds, finely chopped
2/3 cup granulated sugar
1 cup cold butter
1 tablespoon water
1/2 cup raspberry jam
1/2 cup almonds, slivered

Combine flour, chopped almonds and granulated sugar. Cut in butter until mixture resembles coarse crumbs. Add water; form dough into ball. Cover and refrigerate for 1 hour.

On a floured surface, roll dough to 1/8 inch thickness; cut with 2-inch round cookie cutter. Place on greased cookie sheets and bake in preheated oven at 350 degrees F for 7 to 10 minutes. When cool, spread 1/2 teaspoon jam on half the cookies; top with second cookie to make sandwich. Spread tops of cookies with frosting; top with slivered almonds placed in petal-like design.

Frosting:

2 squares (1-oz. each) unsweetened chocolate
2/3 cup confectioners' sugar
4 tablespoons butter, softened

Melt chocolate in microwave for 20 seconds or until melted. Let cool. Beat chocolate, confectioners' sugar and butter until smooth.

Yield: 2 dozen cookies.

Ice Box St. Nick Cookies

For the holidays, you can't go wrong with these crisp cookies. The dough can be stored in the refrigerator for a few days and cookies sliced off and baked any time fresh cookies are needed.

1/2 cup margarine or butter, softened
1/2 cup vegetable oil
3/4 cup granulated sugar
3/4 cup brown sugar, packed
1 egg, beaten
2 cups all-purpose flour
1 1/2 teaspoons cinnamon
1/2 teaspoon nutmeg
1/2 teaspoon baking soda
1/2 teaspoon allspice
1/2 teaspoon cloves
1/2 teaspoon baking powder
1/2 cup pecans, chopped fine

Cream margarine or butter, oil, granulated sugar and brown sugar. Add egg. In another bowl, combine flour, cinnamon, nutmeg, baking soda, allspice, cloves and baking powder. Combine flour mixture and butter mixture; add nuts. Shape into roll, wrap in waxed paper and chill in refrigerator overnight. Slice and bake in preheated oven at 350 degrees F about 10 minutes.

Yield: 5 1/2 dozen cookies.

Chocolate Christmas Cookies

This decadent chocolaty cookie has a surprise Rolo® candy inside.

1 cup margarine or butter, softened
1 cup granulated sugar
1 cup brown sugar, packed
2 eggs
2 teaspoons vanilla
2 1/2 cups all-purpose flour
3/4 cup cocoa
1 teaspoon baking soda
48 Rolo® candies
1/2 cup pecans, chopped
1/4 cup granulated sugar (for rolling)
1 cup white chocolate chips

Cream margarine or butter, granulated sugar, brown sugar, eggs and vanilla, beating well. Stir in flour, cocoa and baking soda. Refrigerate dough in refrigerator for 4 hours or overnight.

Wrap dough around Rolo® candy pieces to form a ball. Roll ball into mixture of chopped pecans and granulated sugar. Place on greased cookie sheet and bake in preheated oven at 375 degrees F for 8 to 10 minutes. Do not overbake. Cool. Melt white chocolate chips and drizzle over cooled cookies.

Yield: 4 dozen.

Candy Cane Cookies

These cookies look so festive on a holiday cookie tray. Try using different colors for different holidays, such as orange, green, yellow, etc.

1 cup margarine, softened
1 cup confectioners' sugar
1 1/2 teaspoon almond flavoring
1 teaspoon vanilla extract
1 egg
2 1/2 cups all-purpose flour
1 teaspoon salt
Red food coloring

Mix together margarine, confectioners' sugar, almond flavoring, vanilla and egg. Mix flour and salt together; add to sugar mixture. Divide dough in half. Add red food coloring to one half.

Take one ball of each color and roll into long ropes. Twist ropes of each color together to make "barber pole" stripes. Shape into candy canes. Sprinkle granulated sugar on cookies and bake in preheated oven at 375 degrees F for 9 minutes.

Yield: 4 dozen cookies.

Oatmeal Cookies
Refrigerated Cookies

These cookies don't require a lot of fuss but still have terrific flavor.

1 cup margarine, softened
1/2 cup brown sugar, packed
1/2 cup granulated sugar
2 cups all-purpose flour
1/2 teaspoon baking soda
1/4 teaspoon salt
1 1/2 cups quick oats

Cream margarine, brown sugar and granulated sugar together. In another bowl, mix together flour, baking soda and salt. Add flour mixture to sugar mixture; add quick oats.

Shape dough in rolls and refrigerate for 4 hours or overnight. Then cut into 1/4" slices. Bake in preheated oven at 350 degrees F 10 to 12 minutes or until lightly brown.

Yield: 2 dozen cookies.

Soothing Cookies

Make these cookies when you are feeling stressed – take the stress out on the dough and make a fabulous cookie.

1 cup butter or margarine, softened
1 cup brown sugar, packed
1 cup all-purpose flour
2 cups quick oats
1 teaspoon baking soda

In a large bowl, cream butter or margarine and brown sugar together. Add flour, oats and baking soda and mix well.

Now mash, knead and squeeze the dough. The longer you abuse the dough, the better the cookies taste.

Form the dough into small balls. Place on ungreased cookie sheets. Using a small glass, butter the bottom, dip in granulated sugar each time and press the cookies flat. Bake in preheated oven at 350 degrees F for 10 to 12 minutes.

Yield: 4 dozen.

Crisp Oatmeal Cookies

These crisp cookies are fabulous! Great for after-school snacks too.

1/2 cup margarine or butter, softened
1 egg
1/4 teaspoon vanilla
1/2 cup granulated sugar
1/2 cup brown sugar, packed
1 cup all-purpose flour
1/2 teaspoon baking powder
1/2 teaspoon baking soda
1/4 teaspoon salt
3/4 cup quick oats
1/4 cup walnuts, chopped

Mix margarine or butter, egg and vanilla together. Add granulated sugar and brown sugar; mix well. In a separate bowl, combine flour, baking powder, baking soda and salt. Stir in oats and nuts. Roll in small balls, dip in sugar. Bake in preheated oven at 375 degrees F for 10 to 12 minutes.

Yield: 1 1/2 dozen cookies.

Grandma's Oatmeal Cookies

Create your own variation of this cookie by adding 2 cups of chocolate or other flavored chips to the sugar mixture.

1 cup brown sugar, packed
1 cup granulated sugar
1 cup margarine, softened
2 eggs, beaten
1 teaspoon vanilla
1 1/2 cups all-purpose flour
1 teaspoon baking soda
1 teaspoon salt
3 cups quick oats
1/2 cup pecans, chopped

In a large bowl, combine brown sugar, granulated sugar, margarine, eggs and vanilla. In another bowl, mix flour, baking soda and salt. Add flour mixture to sugar mixture; mix well. Form into a log and wrap in plastic wrap. Refrigerate for 4 hours or overnight. Slice and bake on cookie sheets in preheated oven at 350 degrees F for 10 minutes.

Yield: 4 to 5 dozen cookies.

Bar Cookies

Chewy Granola Bars

These chewy bars are loaded with chopped nuts, dried fruit and more healthy ingredients.

1 cup brown sugar, packed
1/2 cup butter, melted
1/2 cup light corn syrup
2/3 cups peanut butter
3 cups quick oats
2 teaspoons vanilla
1/3 cup wheat germ
1/2 cup sunflower seeds
1/2 cup raisins or dried cherries
1 cup nuts, chopped

Cream brown sugar, butter and corn syrup. Mix in peanut butter, oats, vanilla, wheat germ, sunflower seeds, raisins or dried cherries and nuts. Press into a greased or buttered 9x13" baking dish. Bake in preheated oven at 350 degrees F for 15 to 20 minutes.

Yield: 12 granola bars.

Chocolate Cheesecake Bars

Classic cheesecake as an easy bar cookie with chocolate added to the crust.

1/3 cup butter
1 (11-ounce) package milk chocolate chips
2 cups graham cracker crumbs
1 (8-ounce) package cream cheese, softened
1 (14-ounce) can sweetened condensed milk
1 egg
1 teaspoon vanilla

Melt butter and chocolate chips in microwave, stirring every 20 to 30 seconds until melted. Remove from microwave and add graham cracker crumbs. Spray a 9 x 13 inch baking dish with non-stick cooking spray. Press half the graham cracker mixture in the baking dish.

In a separate bowl, with an electric mixer, beat cream cheese until light and fluffy. Add sweetened condensed milk, egg and vanilla. Pour into baking dish. Add the remaining graham cracker crumb mixture on top. Bake in preheated oven at 350 degrees F for 25 to 30 minutes. When cool, cut into bars.

Yield: 2 dozen.

Chocolate Cherry Bars

These bars are a rich, chewy cookie. This recipe makes enough for 2 8x8" baking dishes.

1 1/2 cups granulated sugar
1 1/2 teaspoons salt
5 eggs
1 1/2 teaspoons vanilla
1 cup cake flour
1/2 cup vegetable oil
1/4 cup margarine, melted
3 1/2 squares (1 oz. each) unsweetened chocolate, melted
1 1/2 cups shredded coconut
1 1/2 cups candied cherries, chopped

Beat granulated sugar, salt, eggs and vanilla until mixture is light and fluffy. Add flour; mix well. Add vegetable oil, margarine and chocolate. Fold in coconut and cherries.

Spray the sides and bottom of 2 8x8" baking dishes with non-stick cooking spray. Pour half of the mixture in each dish and bake in preheated oven at 350 degrees F for 45 minutes.

Yield: 64 bars.

Crispy Cookie Bars

1/2 cup butter or margarine, softened
3/4 cup granulated sugar
2 eggs, beaten
1 teaspoon vanilla
3/4 cup all-purpose flour
2 tablespoons cocoa
1/4 teaspoon salt
1/4 teaspoon baking powder
1/2 cup chopped nuts, optional
2 cups mini marshmallows
1-6 oz. pkg. chocolate chips
1/2 cup peanut butter
1 1/2 cups crispy rice cereal (as Rice Krispies)

In a small bowl, cream butter or margarine and granulated sugar. Add eggs and vanilla. In another bowl, mix flour, cocoa, salt and baking powder; stir flour mixture into creamed mixture. Add nuts, if desired. Spread in a 9x13" baking dish. Bake in preheated oven at 350 degrees F for 15 minutes.

Remove from oven and scatter mini marshmallows on top; return to oven for 3 minutes, then cool. In heavy saucepan over low heat, melt the chocolate chips and peanut butter (or melt in microwave, stirring and checking frequently). Stir the cereal into the chocolate mixture and spread over cooled bars. Refrigerate.

Yield: 18 to 24 bars.

Scotch Shortbread

These rich buttery cookies only have 5 ingredients so they are a breeze to make when company's coming.

1/2 lb. butter, softened (no substitutes)
3/4 cup confectioners' sugar
3/4 teaspoon vanilla
1/2 teaspoon lemon juice
2 cups + 2 tablespoons all-purpose flour

Cream together butter, confectioners' sugar, vanilla and lemon juice. Work flour into creamed mixture until it forms a ball. Roll out or pat with hands to one-half inch thick on a lightly buttered cookie sheet. Bake in preheated oven at 325 degrees F for 25 minutes or until lightly browned. Cut into squares or desired shapes while hot.

Yield: 40 squares.

Coffee Brownies

A rich creamy fudgy chocolate brownie treat that could always be made even richer with chocolate frosting!

2 1/2 cups brown sugar, packed
3/4 cup butter or margarine
2 teaspoons strong instant coffee granules
1 teaspoon hot water
2 eggs
2 teaspoons vanilla
2 cups all-purpose flour
2 teaspoons baking powder
1/2 teaspoon salt
1 cup pecans, chopped
1 cup chocolate chips

In a medium saucepan, melt brown sugar and butter or margarine over medium heat until melted, stirring constantly. Dissolve coffee granules in hot water; blend into sugar mixture and let cool. Beat in eggs and vanilla.

In a separate bowl, combine flour, baking powder and salt; stir flour mixture into sugar mixture. Stir in pecans and chocolate chips. Spread in a buttered or greased 9x13" baking dish. Bake in preheated oven at 350 degrees F for 30 minutes.

Yield: 2 dozen.

Fruit Cocktail Bars

These are one of my favorite bar cookies. So moist and rich, can't beat them!

1 1/4 cups all-purpose flour
1/4 teaspoon salt
1 teaspoon baking soda
1/2 teaspoon baking powder
1-8 oz. can fruit cocktail with juice
1/2 teaspoon vanilla
1 egg

Topping:
1 1/2 cups brown sugar, packed
1/2 teaspoon vanilla
2 tablespoons butter or margarine, melted
1/2 cup pecans or walnuts, finely chopped

Combine flour, salt, baking soda and baking powder. Stir in fruit cocktail with juice and vanilla. Add egg; mix well. Spray a 9x13" baking dish lightly with non-stick cooking spray. Pour batter into baking dish.

Mix all topping ingredients together. Sprinkle topping over bars. Bake in preheated oven at 350 degrees F for 40 to 45 minutes.

Yield: 20 bars.

To Die for Bars

This rich bar cookie is one of my favorites. It is not only delicious, but freezes and travels well also.

1/2 cup margarine or butter
1 cup graham crackers, crushed
1 1/2 cups chocolate chips
1 cup flaked coconut
1 cup pecans, chopped
1 cup sweetened condensed milk

Melt margarine or butter and put in a 9x13" baking dish. Add graham cracker crumbs on top of butter and press into dish. Sprinkle on the chocolate chips, then coconut, then pecan pieces.

Pour sweetened condensed milk over all. Bake in preheated oven at 350 degrees F for 25 to 30 minutes. Cut into squares when cool.

Yield: 24 squares.

Butterscotch Squares

If you like butterscotch, you will love this tasty treat.

1 cup butter or margarine, softened
1 cup brown sugar, packed
1 cup granulated sugar
2 eggs, beaten
1 1/2 cups all-purpose flour
2 teaspoons baking powder
2 teaspoons vanilla
1/2 cup pecans or walnuts

In a large bowl, cream butter or margarine, brown sugar and granulated sugar. Mix in eggs and vanilla. Combine flour and baking powder; add flour mixture to sugar mixture. Cover bottom of 9x13" greased pan with nuts. Pour mixture over nuts and bake in preheated oven at 350 degrees F for 20 to 30 minutes.

Yield: 20 bars.

Three Layer Cookies

These cookie bars are so sweet and tasty. The 3 layers may require a bit more work, but they are well worth it.

First Layer:

1/2 cup butter, softened
1/4 cup granulated sugar
1/3 cup cocoa
1 teaspoon vanilla
1 egg, slightly beaten
2 cups graham cracker crumbs
1 cup grated coconut
1/2 cup nuts, chopped

Combine butter, granulated sugar, cocoa and vanilla in a double boiler and cook until blended. Add egg and cook 5 minutes, stirring constantly. Add graham cracker crumbs, coconut and nuts. Press in 9x13" baking dish and let cool.

Second Layer

1/2 cup butter, softened
3 tablespoons milk
2 teaspoons vanilla
1 package instant vanilla pudding mix
2 cups confectioners' sugar

Cream butter. Mix milk, vanilla and pudding; add to butter. Add sugar gradually; beat until smooth. Spread over first layer. Let set until firm.

Third Layer:

4 oz. semi-sweet chocolate chips
1 tablespoon butter

Melt chocolate with butter and spread on top.

Yield: 20 bars.

Peanut Butter Granola Bars

This chewy granola bar recipe is one of my favorites.

1 1/2 cups old fashioned rolled oats
1/4 cup pecan pieces
1 tablespoon chia seeds
1/2 cup natural peanut butter, melted
1/4 cup honey
1/2 cup dried cherries
1/4 cup chocolate chips

In a large bowl, combine oats, pecans and chia seeds. Melt peanut butter in microwave for 1 minute. Add peanut butter and honey to oat mixture and mix until well moistened. Fold in cherries and chocolate chips. If dough is still too dry, add more peanut butter or honey 1 tablespoon at a time until moistened. Line an 8x8" baking dish with parchment paper, leaving a few inches at 2 ends to be used as "handles". Spray parchment paper with non-stick cooking spray. Press dough very firmly in dish. Bake in preheated oven at 350 degrees F for 18 to 20 minutes.

To cut into bars: Measure where you will want to cut the bars. Score bars lightly where they will be cut. Let bars cool completely, then refrigerate for 1/2 hour. Remove bars using the "handles" of the parchment paper. Using a non-serrated knife, run knife under hot water, dry on a clean towel and cut a complete row at a time. Repeat until all bars are cut.

Yield: 12 granola bars.

Peanut Butter Granola Bars

Apple Bars

Sliced apples, combined with butter and cinnamon, create a chewy delicious cookie.

1 cup all-purpose flour
1 cup quick oats
1/2 cup brown sugar, packed
1/2 teaspoon salt
1/2 teaspoon baking soda
1/2 teaspoon cinnamon
1/2 cup butter or margarine
2 1/2 cups apples, sliced
2 tablespoons margarine
1/2 cup walnuts
1/4 cup granulated sugar

In a large bowl, mix together flour, oats, brown sugar, salt, baking soda and cinnamon. Cut in the butter or margarine until the mixture is crumbly and coarse.

Grease the bottom of an 8 or 9 inch baking dish. Spread half the oats mixture in the bottom of the baking dish. Dot the surface of the oats mixture with 2 tablespoons of margarine; evenly spread the sliced apples in the baking dish. Sprinkle the top with walnuts and granulated sugar. Finish by adding the remaining half of the oats mixture on top. Bake in preheated oven at 350 degrees F for 40 to 45 minutes.

Yield: 12 bars.

Butter Cookies

Crisp Butter Cookies

Delicious butter cookies with texture, thanks to the crispy rice cereal and nuts.

1 cup butter, softened (no substitutes)
1 cup granulated sugar
1 3/4 cups all-purpose flour
1 teaspoon salt
1/2 teaspoon baking powder
1/2 teaspoon baking soda
3/4 cup crispy rice cereal (as Rice Krispies)
1/2 cup nuts, chopped

Cream butter and granulated sugar together. Add flour, salt, baking powder and baking soda. Fold in rice cereal and nuts. Shape into balls and press down on greased cookie sheet. Bake in preheated oven at 325 degrees F for 10 to 15 minutes.

Yield: 2 dozen cookies.

Dutch Butter Cookies

This buttery rich cookie will melt in your mouth. Just a few cookies may be baked at one time and the remainder of the dough stored in the refrigerator, if you prefer.

1 cup butter, softened
1 cup granulated sugar
2 cups all-purpose flour
1/4 cup water
1/4 teaspoon vanilla
1/4 teaspoon baking soda

Cream the butter, blend in granulated sugar, and add flour. Add vanilla and baking soda to 1/4 cup water, pour over first mixture and stir with spoon until the sides of the bowl are clean.

Form into a roll on waxed paper. Chill in refrigerator for 4 hours or overnight. When thoroughly chilled, slice with sharp, thin-bladed knife into thin slices; place on greased cookie sheet, and bake in preheated oven at 350 degrees F for 10 to 12 minutes or until lightly browned.

Yield: 3 dozen cookies.

Butter Cookies

These easy to make cookies come out so good and buttery.

1 cup granulated sugar
1/2 cup vegetable oil
1/2 cup butter, softened
2 egg yolks
2 cups all-purpose flour
1/2 teaspoon baking soda
1/8 teaspoon salt

Combine granulated sugar, vegetable oil, butter and egg yolks together. Mix together flour, baking soda and salt; add to sugar mixture and mix well. Roll into balls. Using a small glass, butter the bottom, dip in granulated sugar each time and press the cookies flat. Bake on cookie sheets in preheated oven at 350 degrees F for 10 to 12 minutes.

Yield: 2 dozen cookies.

Sand Butter Cookies

Optionally, one cup of chopped walnuts may be added to this cookie.

1/3 cup granulated sugar
1 cup butter, softened
2 teaspoons water
1 teaspoon vanilla
2 cups all-purpose flour
Confectioners' sugar

Cream granulated sugar and butter. Add water and vanilla. Blend in flour, chill in refrigerator 4 hours or overnight. Shape into balls. Bake in preheated oven on ungreased cookie sheet at 325 degrees F for about 20 minutes. Cool slightly. Roll in confectioners' sugar.

Yield: 3 dozen cookies.

Nut Cookies

Almond Cookies

A blanched almond is merely an almond with the skin removed. You can purchase skinless almonds in the baking aisle or blanch the almonds yourself.

1 1/3 cups blanched almonds
2/3 cup granulated sugar
1/8 teaspoon salt
2 egg whites

Blend blanched almonds in blender until a fine consistency. Mix with granulated sugar and salt. With an electric mixer, beat egg whites until they form stiff peaks. Fold into almond mixture. Drop heaping teaspoonfuls onto a greased cookie sheet. Bake in preheated oven at 400 degrees F for about 10 minutes (until cookies are light brown on top). Remove to rack and cool.

Yield: 15 to 18 cookies.

Macadamia Dutch Butter Slices

The poppy seeds are mixed right into the dough, making an interesting looking cookie. So rich and buttery.

1 cup butter, softened
1 cup granulated sugar
1 egg yolk
1 1/2 cups macadamia nuts, chopped
1/2 cup poppy seeds
1/2 teaspoon ground cinnamon
1/2 teaspoon ground ginger
1 teaspoon vanilla
1/4 teaspoon salt
2 1/2 cups all-purpose flour

Separate egg and discard white. Cream butter and granulated sugar together and add egg yolk. Stir in macadamia nuts, poppy seeds, cinnamon, ginger, vanilla and salt. Gradually add enough flour to make a firm but sticky dough (may not need all of the 2 1/2 cups). Do not knead or work dough after all of flour has been added.

Form dough into rolls 1 1/2" inches in diameter and wrap in wax paper. Refrigerate for 4 hours or until rolls are firm. When firm, cut rolls into 1/4" slices. Spread them slightly apart on ungreased cookie sheets. Bake in preheated oven at 325 degrees F for 12 minutes or until cookies are sand-colored.

Yield: 4 dozen cookies.

Cashew Cookies

Cashews and sour cream make for an irresistible cookie.

1 cup brown sugar, packed
1/2 cup butter or margarine, softened
1/2 teaspoon vanilla
1 egg
2 cups all-purpose flour
1/4 teaspoon salt
3/4 teaspoon baking soda
3/4 teaspoon baking powder
1/2 cup sour cream
1 3/4 cups salted cashews, chopped

In a large bowl, combine brown sugar, butter or margarine, vanilla and egg. In another bowl, mix flour, salt, baking soda and baking powder. Add flour mixture to sugar mixture; mix well. Add sour cream and cashews; mix well.

Drop by teaspoon on greased cookie sheet. Bake in preheated oven at 375 degrees F for 10 minutes.

Yield: 2 dozen cookies.

Walnut Cluster Cookies

These cookies showcase the nutty flavor of walnuts.

1/4 cup butter, softened
1/2 cup granulated sugar
1 egg, beaten
2 squares (1-oz. each) semi-sweet baking chocolate
1 1/2 cups all-purpose flour
1/4 teaspoon baking powder
1/2 teaspoon salt
1 teaspoon vanilla
2 cups walnuts, broken into large pieces

Cream butter and granulated sugar. Add egg and mix. Melt chocolate in microwave and add to egg mixture. In another bowl, combine flour, baking powder and salt; add to sugar mixture and mix well. Add vanilla and nuts. Drop by spoonful on greased cookie sheet. Bake in preheated oven at 350 degrees F for 12 minutes.

Yield: 2 dozen cookies.

Pecan Snickerdoodles

Here's a famous traditional cookie with pecans added. A soft and delicious cookie.

1 1/2 cups granulated sugar
1 cup butter or margarine, softened
2 eggs
2 1/2 cups all-purpose flour
1 teaspoon baking soda
2 teaspoons cream of tartar
1/4 teaspoon salt
1 tablespoon cinnamon
2 tablespoons granulated sugar
36 pecan halves

Cream together butter or margarine and granulated sugar. Mix in eggs and beat until fluffy and light. Combine flour, baking soda, cream of tartar and salt; add to sugar mixture. Mix until blended. Refrigerate for 1 hour or until chilled.

Shape into 1-inch balls. Roll in mixture of cinnamon and granulated sugar. Place 2 inches apart on ungreased cookie sheets and in the center of each ball press in a pecan half. Bake in preheated oven at 400 degrees F for 10 to 12 minutes or until lightly browned.

Yield: 3 dozen cookies.

Salted Peanut Cookies

This tasty cookie is a perfect "peanut lovers" cookie.

1 cup butter or margarine, softened
2 cups brown sugar, packed
1 tablespoon sour cream
1 teaspoon vanilla
2 eggs, beaten
2 1/2 cups all-purpose flour
1 teaspoon baking soda
1 teaspoon baking powder
1 cup cornflakes
1 1/2 cups salted peanuts

Cream butter or margarine and brown sugar. Add sour cream, vanilla and eggs. In a separate bowl, mix together flour, baking soda and baking powder. Add to sugar mixture, then add cornflakes; mix well. Stir in nuts.

Drop by teaspoonful on well-greased or parchment-lined cookie sheets. Flatten slightly. Bake in preheated oven at 350 degrees F for 12 to 15 minutes.

Yield: 4 dozen cookies.

Walnut Spice Kisses

Super easy cookie to mix together and your house will smell heavenly while they are baking.

1 egg white
1/8 teaspoon salt
1/4 cup granulated sugar
1 teaspoon cinnamon
1/8 teaspoon nutmeg
1/2 cup coconut
1 cup walnuts, finely chopped
24 walnut halves

Using an electric mixer, beat egg white with salt until stiff. Gradually beat in granulated sugar, cinnamon and nutmeg. Fold in coconut and walnuts. Drop by teaspoonful on greased cookie sheet. Top with walnut halves. Bake in preheated oven at 250 degrees F for 35 to 40 minutes.

Yield: 2 dozen cookies.

Pecan Puffs

Instead of rolling these pecan puffs in confectioners' sugar, try placing the sugar in a brown paper bag and adding the cookies a few at a time, shaking the bag to coat the cookies.

1 cup margarine, softened
1/2 cup confectioners' sugar
2 1/4 cups all-purpose flour
1/2 teaspoon salt
1 teaspoon vanilla
3/4 cup pecans, chopped

Cream margarine and confectioners' sugar. Stir in flour, salt, vanilla and pecans. Mix well. Roll into balls about 1-inch in diameter and place on greased cookie sheet. Bake in preheated oven at 375 degrees F for 12 to 15 minutes. While cookies are still warm, roll them in confectioners' sugar.

Yield: 2 1/2 dozen cookies.

Refrigerator Cookies

Bran Refrigerator Cookies

These sweet bran and nut cookies will make a nice, hearty snack.

1 cup margarine or butter, softened
2 cups brown sugar, packed
1 egg
3 cups all-purpose flour
2 teaspoons baking powder
1 cup whole bran cereal
1 cup nuts, chopped

Cream together the margarine or butter, brown sugar and egg until fluffy. In a separate bowl, mix flour and baking powder; stir in cereal and nuts. Add to sugar mixture; stir until moistened. Line a loaf pan with wax paper and press dough evenly into it. Refrigerate overnight. Slice 1/4 inch or less thick and cut slices in half. Bake on ungreased cookie sheets in preheated oven at 400 degrees F for 8 to 10 minutes.

Yield: 4 dozen cookies.

Date Pinwheel Cookie

You may recognize these cookies as something close to what your grandmother used to bake.

1/2 cup margarine or butter, softened
1/2 cup granulated sugar
1/2 cup brown sugar, packed
1 egg
2 cups all-purpose flour
1 teaspoon baking soda
1/4 teaspoon salt

Filling:
1/2 lb. dates, chopped
2/3 cup water
1/4 cup granulated sugar

Filling: Simmer dates with granulated sugar and water until tender.

Cream together margarine or butter, granulated sugar and brown sugar. Add egg and mix well. In a separate bowl, mix together flour, baking soda and salt. Add flour mixture to sugar mixture. Form dough into a ball and refrigerate for at least one hour. Roll dough out on a well-floured surface to be a thin sheet about 1/4" thick. Spread with date filling. Roll up in a "jelly roll" fashion. Refrigerate or freeze for at least one hour. Slice into 1/4" thick pieces and bake in preheated oven at 350 degrees F for 10 to 12 minutes.

Yield: 2 dozen cookies.

Toffee Cookies

If you like Heath candy bars, you will love these cookies.

1 1/2 cups margarine or butter, softened
1 1/2 cups granulated sugar
2 teaspoons vanilla
3 cups all-purpose flour
1/2 teaspoon baking soda
5-1.4 oz. toffee candy bars (as Heath bars)

Cream together margarine or butter, granulated sugar and vanilla. In a separate bowl, combine flour and baking soda; add to sugar mixture and mix well. Stir in 5 large, crushed Heath bars (crush in Ziploc bag with hammer).

Make 2 rolls of dough. Refrigerate for 4 hours or until thoroughly chilled. Slice, place on parchment-lined cookie sheets and bake in preheated oven for 14 to 18 minutes at 325 degrees F.

Yield: 5 dozen cookies.

Three In One Cookies

Dividing the dough into thirds and using a different ingredient in each results in three different cookies. One third contains coconut, one third uses pecans and the last third has raisins.

1 cup butter or margarine, slightly softened
1/2 cup brown sugar, packed
1/2 cup granulated sugar
1/2 teaspoon vanilla
1 egg
2 cups all-purpose flour
1/2 teaspoon baking soda
1/4 teaspoon salt
1/2 cup flaked coconut
1/2 cup pecans, chopped
1/2 cup raisins

Cream butter or margarine, brown sugar and granulated sugar together until light and fluffy. Stir in vanilla and egg; beat until smooth. In a separate bowl, combine flour, baking soda and salt. Add flour mixture to sugar mixture; mix well.

Divide the dough into 3 bowls. Mix coconut into one, pecans into the second one and raisins into the third one. Shape dough from each bowl into 2 rolls, 1 inch across, and wrap in plastic wrap, foil or waxed paper. Twist the ends to seal tightly. Refrigerate for 4 hours or overnight. To bake, cut in thin slices. Bake on greased cookie sheets in preheated oven at 375 degrees F for 8 minutes until lightly browned.

Yield: 6 dozen cookies.

Oatmeal Refrigerator Cookies

A thin sharp knife works best for slicing the cookie roll. Thin slices result in a crisp cookie, whereas thicker slices will make a chewier cookie.

1 cup margarine, softened
1 cup granulated sugar
1 cup brown sugar, packed
2 eggs, well beaten
1 teaspoon vanilla
1 1/2 cups all-purpose flour
1 teaspoon baking soda
1 1/2 teaspoons salt
3 cups quick oats

In a large bowl, cream margarine, granulated sugar and brown sugar. Beat until light and fluffy. Beat in eggs and vanilla. In a separate bowl, combine flour, baking soda and salt. Add flour mixture to sugar mixture; mix in oats. Shape into rolls 2 inches across and wrap in plastic wrap, foil or waxed paper. Twist the ends to seal them tightly.

Refrigerate for 4 hours or overnight. To bake, cut in thin slices. Bake on ungreased cookie sheets in preheated oven at 400 degrees F for 8 minutes.

Yield: 6 dozen cookies.

Chocolate Cookies

Chocolate Chunk Cookies

Indulge your chocolate cravings with a cookie full of nuts and chocolate pieces.

2-8 oz. packages semi-sweet baking chocolate squares, divided
3/4 cup brown sugar, packed
2 eggs
1/4 cup butter or margarine, softened
1 teaspoon vanilla
1/2 cup all-purpose flour
1/4 teaspoon baking powder
2 cups nuts, chopped

Coarsely chop one of the packages of chocolate squares and set aside. In a microwave, melt the other package of the chocolate squares. Blend in brown sugar, eggs, butter or margarine and vanilla. Combine flour and baking powder; add to mixture.

Mix in chopped chocolate squares and nuts. Drop by heaping tablespoonfuls of dough onto ungreased cookie sheet. Bake in preheated oven at 350 degrees F for 10 to 12 minutes or until cookies are puffy.

Yield: 1 1/2 dozen.

Chocolate Mint Cookies

These cookies are big on chocolate flavor and look so pretty that no one will guess how easy they are to make.

3/4 cup brown sugar, packed
1/4 cup and 2 tablespoons margarine or butter
1 tablespoon water
1 cup semisweet chocolate chips
1 egg
1 1/4 cups all-purpose flour
1/2 teaspoon baking soda
1/4 teaspoon salt
1 package (4.7 oz.) chocolate-covered thin mints (28 mints)
(Andes Mints)

In a saucepan, combine brown sugar, margarine or butter and water. Cook over medium heat until butter or margarine is melted, stirring occasionally. Remove pan from heat, stir in chocolate chips until melted and let cool for 15 minutes.

Pour mixture into a large bowl, and beat in egg. In a separate bowl, combine flour, baking soda and salt; add to chocolate mixture. Refrigerate dough for at least 1/2 hour or until chilled.

Roll dough into 1-inch balls and place 2 inches apart on greased or parchment paper-lined cookie sheets. Bake in preheated oven at 350 degrees F for 8 to 10 minutes. When cookies are finished baking, immediately press a chocolate covered mint into the top of each cookie and let sit about a minute until mint is softened. Using the back of a spoon, swirl the mint, making a pattern with the green filling of the mint wafer.

Yield: 2 1/2 dozen cookies.

Double Chocolate Cookies

This cookie batter is swimming in melted chocolate and chocolate chips, producing a cookie that is bursting with chocolate flavor.

6 oz. pkg. semi-sweet chocolate chips
1/2 cup margarine or butter, softened
1/2 cup granulated sugar
1 cup flour
1/2 teaspoon salt
1/2 teaspoon baking soda
1 egg
1/4 cup warm water
1/2 cup nuts, chopped

Melt one half of the chocolate chips in a microwave on 50% power. Let cool.

In a large bowl, cream margarine or butter and granulated sugar. Stir in unbeaten egg and cooled melted chocolate. In a separate bowl, mix flour, salt and baking soda. Add flour mixture and water to the sugar mixture; mix well. Stir in nuts and remaining chocolate chips; drop by teaspoonful on ungreased cookie sheets. Bake in preheated oven at 350 degrees F for 12 to 15 minutes.

Yield: 3 dozen.

Chocolate Drop Cookies

An easy cookie that is tasty and full of chocolate goodness.

2 eggs, beaten
2 cups brown sugar, packed
2 teaspoons vanilla
1 cup margarine, softened
3 cups all-purpose flour
1/2 teaspoon salt
1 teaspoon baking soda
1/4 cup cocoa
1 cup whole milk
1/2 cup nuts, chopped

Beat eggs and brown sugar until light and fluffy; add vanilla and margarine. Blend well. In a separate bowl, mix flour, salt, baking soda and cocoa; add to sugar mixture alternately with whole milk. Stir in nuts. Drop by teaspoonfuls onto greased cookie sheet. Bake in preheated oven at 350 degrees F for 8 to 10 minutes.

Yield: 4 1/2 dozen cookies.

Excellent Chocolate Cookies

This is my favorite chocolate cookie. Be sure to bake only for 10 minutes.

2 tablespoons butter
1 1/2 cups of chocolate chips
1 cup all-purpose flour
1-14 oz. can sweetened condensed milk
1 cup pecans

Melt butter and chocolate chips in microwave. Mix with flour, sweetened condensed milk and pecans.

Drop on greased cookie sheet and flatten a little. Bake exactly 10 minutes in preheated oven at 325 degrees F.

Yield: 2 dozen cookies.

Chocolate Puff Cookies

This is a macaroon-style chocolate cookie.

2 egg whites
1/2 cup granulated sugar
1/4 teaspoon salt
1 teaspoon vanilla
1-6 oz. pkg. semi-sweet chocolate chips, melted
1 1/3 cups coconut
1/2 cup walnuts, chopped

With an electric mixer, beat egg whites until stiff. Add granulated sugar gradually to egg whites and beat until mixed. Add salt and vanilla. Mix in chocolate, coconut and nuts. Drop by teaspoonfuls on cookie sheets sprayed with non-stick cooking spray. Bake in preheated oven at 300 degrees F for 10 to 15 minutes.

Yield: 3 dozen cookies.

No-Bake Cookies

Simple Cookies

You will be surprised at how fast you can whip up a batch of these cookies.
Note: 1/4 lb. of soda crackers is 1 sleeve of crackers or 40 crackers.

2 cups granulated sugar
3/4 cup milk
1/4 lb. crushed soda crackers
6 tablespoons peanut butter
1 teaspoon vanilla

In a saucepan, combine granulated sugar and milk. Bring to a boil over medium heat and boil for 3 minutes, stirring constantly. Remove from heat. Add crackers, peanut butter and vanilla; mix well. Drop by teaspoonfuls on waxed paper.

Yield: 1 dozen cookies.

Moon Ball Cookies

This no-bake cookie mixes up quickly with only a few ingredients and will also freeze well. To make cocoa balls, add 1/4 cup of cocoa.

1 cup nonfat dry milk
1/2 cup natural peanut butter
1/2 cup honey (a little less than 1/2 cup)
1/2 cup crushed granola or crushed cereal flakes

Combine nonfat dry milk, peanut butter and honey. Form into 1-inch balls and roll in crushed granola or crushed cereal flakes.

Yield: 3 dozen.

Coconut Cookies

These cookies use light cream which you should be able to find in the store labeled as such. It is table cream or coffee cream.

2 cups granulated sugar
1 cup brown sugar, packed
1 cup light cream
3 tablespoons light corn syrup
2 1/2 cups flaked coconut

Combine granulated sugar and brown sugar, cream and corn syrup in a heavy saucepan. Bring to a boil over low heat, stirring constantly. Boil gently until a small amount forms a soft ball in cold water. Remove from heat and add coconut. Stir to blend. Beat vigorously until the mixture begins to thicken, about 10 to 20 minutes. Drop by spoonfuls on waxed paper. Let stand until firm.

Yield: 2 dozen cookies.

Almond Bark Cookies

These cookies are very easy to make. Be sure to use white mini-marshmallows, not the colored ones that have fruit flavoring.

12 oz. (1/2 large package) almond bark
2 cups white mini marshmallows
2 cups broken stick pretzels
2 cups crispy rice cereal (as Rice Krispies)
1 or 2 cups dry roasted peanuts

Melt almond bark in double boiler or microwave, stirring every 30 seconds until melted. Add marshmallows, pretzels, rice cereal and peanuts to almond bark; mix well. Drop by spoonfuls on wax paper and cool.

Yield: 3 dozen cookies.

No Bake Brownies

What could be more perfect – quick, chocolate and no bake!

4 cups graham cracker crumbs
1 cup walnuts, chopped
1/2 cup confectioners' sugar
2 cups semi-sweet chocolate chips
1 cup evaporated milk
1 teaspoon vanilla

Combine graham cracker crumbs, walnuts and confectioners' sugar in large bowl. Melt chocolate chips and evaporated milk over low heat; stir constantly. Add vanilla. Reserve 1/2 cup of chocolate mixture and stir remaining chocolate mixture into graham cracker mixture. Spread in greased or buttered 9x9" baking dish. Spread the remaining 1/2 cup chocolate mixture over the top. Refrigerate.

Yield: 2 1/2 dozen cookies.

Corn Flake Cookies

With only 3 ingredients, these cookies are a snap to make.

1 cup peanut butter
2 cups butterscotch chips
6 to 8 cups corn flakes

In a saucepan, melt peanut butter and butterscotch chips. Add corn flakes. Stir together and drop by teaspoons on wax paper or parchment paper. Refrigerate.

Yield: 3 dozen cookies.

Chocolate Cookies

These delicious no-bake cookies are quick and easy to prepare.

1/2 cup milk
5 tablespoons cocoa
2 cups granulated sugar
1/2 cup margarine
3 cups quick oats
1 teaspoon vanilla

In a medium saucepan, mix together milk, cocoa, granulated sugar and margarine. On medium heat, cook for 3 minutes. Add oats and vanilla. Drop on waxed paper. Let stand until firm.

Yield: 2 dozen cookies.

Chow Mein Cookies

This easy and delicious recipe is so easy that it's almost embarrassing to receive so many compliments on them!

1/2 cup peanut butter, chunky
1 cup butterscotch or chocolate chips
1 cup white miniature marshmallows
1-3 oz. can chow mein noodles

In a saucepan over low heat, melt peanut butter and butterscotch or chocolate chips, stirring constantly. (Can also melt in microwave.) Remove from heat; add miniature marshmallows and chow mein noodles. Drop by teaspoonfuls on wax paper or parchment paper. Refrigerate.

Yield: 1 dozen cookies.

Filled Cookies

Candy Bar Cookies

A sweet surprise inside every cookie!

1 cup granulated sugar
1 cup brown sugar, packed
1 cup margarine, softened
2 teaspoons vanilla
2 eggs
1 cup peanut butter
3 cups all-purpose flour
1 teaspoon baking soda
1 teaspoon baking powder
1/2 teaspoon salt
1 lb. bite-size Snicker bars

Cream together granulated sugar, brown sugar, margarine, vanilla and eggs. Add peanut butter. In a separate bowl, combine flour, baking soda, baking powder and salt. Add flour mixture to sugar mixture; mix well. Form dough around candy bar and roll in sugar. Bake on cookie sheets in preheated oven at 350 degrees F for 12 to 15 minutes.

Yield: 4 dozen cookies.

Pocketbook Cookies

These date and nut cookies are easy and delicious.

Cookies:
1/4 cup margarine, softened
3/4 cup granulated sugar
1 egg, beaten
1/4 cup milk
1 teaspoon vanilla
2 1/2 cups all-purpose flour
2 1/4 teaspoons baking powder

Filling:
2 cups dates, cut up
3/4 cup granulated sugar
3/4 cup water
1/2 cup chopped nuts, if desired

FILLING: Combine all ingredients in a medium saucepan. Cook on medium-low heat, stirring constantly, until thickened.

COOKIES: Cream margarine and sugar together. Add egg, milk and vanilla. Combine flour and baking powder with the creamed mixture. Refrigerate for 4 hours or overnight. Roll out dough and cut with round cookie cutter. Spread filling on just half of the cookie and turn over other half of cookie and press sides together. Bake on parchment-lined cookie sheets in preheated oven at 350 degrees F for 10 minutes.

Yield: 4 dozen cookies.

Peanut Butter Thumbprints

The combination of a peanutty cookie paired with chocolate cream cheese is a sweet surprise that's tough to beat.

1/2 cup butter or margarine, softened
1 cup brown sugar, packed
3/4 cup creamy or crunchy peanut butter
1 egg
1/2 teaspoon vanilla extract
1 1/4 cups all-purpose flour
1/2 teaspoon baking powder
1/2 teaspoon baking soda
1 cup unsalted dry roasted peanuts, finely chopped

In a large bowl, beat butter or margarine, brown sugar and peanut butter until well mixed. Add egg and vanilla; beat well. In a separate bowl, mix flour, baking powder and baking soda. Gradually add flour mixture to sugar mixture; mix well.

Shape dough into 1-inch balls; roll in peanuts. Place on ungreased cookie sheet. Bake in preheated oven at 350 degrees F 8 to 10 minutes. Remove from oven and press thumb gently in center of each cookie; cool slightly. Remove from cookie sheet and cool completely. Make thumbprint filling (below). Spoon 1 teaspoon of filling into each thumbprint.

Filling:

1-3 oz. package cream cheese, softened
1/2 teaspoon vanilla
3 tablespoons light corn syrup

1 cup semi-sweet chocolate chips, melted
1/2 cup confectioners' sugar

In a medium bowl, beat cream cheese, vanilla and corn syrup until well mixed. Add chocolate; beat well. Gradually add confectioners' sugar; beating until well mixed and smooth. Yield: 1 1/3 cups filling.

Yield: 4 dozen cookies.

Coconut Cookies

Mystery Coconut Cookies

The mystery in these cookies is the secret ingredients of potato buds and Bisquick.

1/2 cup margarine, softened
1 cup granulated sugar
1 egg
2 teaspoons coconut flavoring
1 1/2 cups potato buds or flakes
1 1/2 cups Bisquick
1/4 to 1/2 cup nuts, chopped

Cream margarine and granulated sugar, add egg and beat well. Add coconut flavoring, potato buds or flakes and Bisquick. Mix well. Drop by teaspoonfuls on greased cookie sheets. Flatten slightly and sprinkle with chopped nuts. Bake in preheated oven at 350 degrees F for 10 to 12 minutes, until edges begin to brown.

Yield: 3 dozen.

Coconut Baboon Cookies

This easy cookie combines moist coconut with chopped nuts for a taste that's nothing to monkey around with.

1/2 cup margarine or butter, softened
1/2 cup granulated sugar
1/2 cup brown sugar, packed
1 cup moist shredded coconut
1/4 cup walnuts, chopped
1 egg
1/2 cup milk
1 1/4 cups all-purpose flour
1/4 teaspoon salt
1/2 teaspoon baking soda

Combine margarine or butter, granulated sugar and brown sugar. Mix in coconut, walnuts, egg and milk. Combine flour, salt and baking soda; add to creamed mixture, mix well. Drop onto greased cookie sheet. Bake in preheated oven at 350 degrees F for 10 to 15 minutes.

Yield: 1-1/2 dozen cookies.

Coconut
Macaroons

A perfect decadent coconut cookie! After baking, these cookies can be drizzled with strips of chocolate or dipped in chocolate. Or topped with green or red candied cherries for the holidays.

5 1/2 cups flaked coconut (a 14-oz. package)
2/3 cup all-purpose flour
1/4 teaspoon salt
1-14 oz. can sweetened condensed milk
1 teaspoon almond extract
1 teaspoon vanilla

Combine coconut, flour and salt. Mix the condensed milk, almond extract and vanilla together; add to coconut mixture. Drop by heaping tablespoonfuls on parchment paper lined cookie sheets. (or foil lined – grease and flour the foil.) Bake in preheated oven at 350 degrees F for 11 to 14 minutes or until coconut is light brown.

Yield: 1-1/2 dozen cookies.

Miscellaneous Cookies

Lace Cookies

These yummy cookies are also delicious dipped in chocolate.

1/2 cup butter or margarine, softened
1 cup granulated sugar
1 teaspoon vanilla
1 egg
2 tablespoons all-purpose flour
1/8 teaspoon of salt
1 cup quick oats

Mix butter or margarine, granulated sugar, vanilla, and egg together. Combine flour and salt; add to sugar mixture. Stir in quick oats. Drop by 1/4 teaspoonful on parchment-lined cookie sheets. Bake in preheated oven at 350 degrees F for 6 to 10 minutes or until edges are light brown. Allow to cool slightly before removing from cookie sheets.

Yield: 5 dozen cookies.

Million Dollar Cookies

These cookies are company-good served with a cup of fresh-brewed coffee.

1 cup margarine, softened
1/2 cup granulated sugar
1/2 cup brown sugar, packed
1 egg
1 teaspoon vanilla
2 cups all-purpose flour
1/2 teaspoon baking soda
1/2 teaspoon salt
1/2 cup nuts, chopped
Granulated sugar
Pecan halves or candied cherries, if desired

Cream margarine, granulated sugar and brown sugar together. Add egg and vanilla, beating well. Mix together flour, baking soda and salt and add to sugar mixture along with nuts.

Form 1-inch balls and roll in granulated sugar. Place dough balls on cookie sheet and press flat with the bottom of a glass dipped in sugar. Add pecan halves or candied cherries, if desired. Bake in preheated oven at 350 degrees F for 10 minutes or until edges turn light brown.

Yield: 3 dozen.

Molasses Cookies

This nice, chewy molasses cookie is full of excellent flavor.

3/4 cup margarine, softened
1 cup granulated sugar
1 egg
1/4 cup molasses, dark
2 cups all-purpose flour
2 teaspoons baking soda
1 teaspoon cinnamon
1/2 teaspoon ginger
1/2 teaspoon salt
1/2 teaspoon cloves

In a large bowl, cream together margarine, granulated sugar, egg and molasses; beat well. In a separate bowl, mix together flour, baking soda, cinnamon, ginger, salt and cloves. Add flour mixture to sugar mixture; mix well. Refrigerate for at least one hour.

Form into 1-inch balls, roll in granulated sugar and place on greased cookie sheets. Bake in preheated oven at 375 degrees F for 8 to 10 minutes.

Yield: 1 dozen cookies.

M&M's Cookies

Instead of using all the M&M's candy in the cookies, just half the candy can be used and the other half used for decorating on top.

1 cup brown sugar, packed
1 cup butter or margarine, softened
1/2 cup granulated sugar
2 teaspoons vanilla
2 eggs
2 1/2 cups all-purpose flour
1 teaspoon baking soda
1 teaspoon salt
1 1/2 cups M&M's milk chocolate candy

Cream brown sugar, butter or margarine, granulated sugar, vanilla and eggs together. In a separate bowl, combine flour, baking soda and salt. Add flour mixture to sugar mixture; mix well.

Stir in M&M's candy. Drop by teaspoonful on ungreased cookie sheet. Bake in preheated oven at 350 degrees F for 10 to 12 minutes.

Yield: 4 dozen cookies.

Special K Cookies

Using a high protein cereal such as Special K gives this cookie a healthy boost.

1 cup margarine, softened
1 cup granulated sugar
1 teaspoon vanilla
1 1/2 cups all-purpose flour
1 teaspoon baking soda
1 teaspoon cream of tartar
1/2 teaspoon salt
2 cups high protein crispy rice and wheat cereal (as Special K)

In a large bowl, cream margarine and granulated sugar. Add vanilla. In another bowl, mix flour, baking soda, cream of tartar and salt. Add flour mixture to sugar mixture; mix well. Stir in cereal. Drop by teaspoonfuls on ungreased cookie sheet. Bake in preheated oven at 350 degrees F until very lightly browned, 12 to 14 minutes.

Yield: 1-1/2 dozen cookies.

Prairie Cookies

This basic old-fashioned cookie enjoys a combination of melted chocolate and walnuts.

4 eggs
2 cups granulated sugar
2 teaspoons vanilla
1/2 cup margarine, softened
4 squares semi-sweet baking chocolate, melted
2 cups all-purpose flour
2 teaspoons baking powder
1 teaspoon salt
1/2 cup walnuts, chopped
Confectioners' sugar

Beat eggs; beat in granulated sugar and vanilla. Blend in margarine and chocolate. In a separate bowl, combine flour, baking powder, salt and walnuts. Add flour mixture to sugar mixture; mix well.

Refrigerate for a few hours or overnight. Shape into 1-inch balls and roll in confectioners' sugar. Place on ungreased cookie sheet. Bake in preheated oven at 350 degrees F for 10 to 15 minutes. Remove from oven before they look done.

Yield: 2 dozen cookies.

Sunflower Seed Cookies

These light and delicate cookies are a little different – nutty and savory-sweet.

1 cup butter or margarine, softened
1 egg
1 cup granulated sugar
1 teaspoon vanilla or 1 teaspoon lemon flavoring
1 1/2 cups all-purpose flour
1/2 teaspoon baking soda
1/2 teaspoon baking powder
1 cup coconut
1 cup sunflower seeds

Combine butter or margarine, egg, granulated sugar and vanilla or lemon flavoring. In a separate bowl, mix flour, baking soda and baking powder together. Add coconut and seeds; mix well. Roll into 1-inch balls and bake on cookie sheets in preheated oven at 325 degrees F for 12 to 15 minutes.

Yield: 2 dozen cookies.

White Drop Cookies

These crisp, buttery treats can be made in no time at all.

1 cup granulated sugar
1 cup butter or margarine, softened
1 teaspoon vanilla
1 egg
2 cups all-purpose flour
1 1/2 teaspoons cream of tartar
1/2 teaspoon salt
1 teaspoon baking soda

Cream granulated sugar and butter or margarine together. Add vanilla and egg. In a separate bowl, combine flour, cream of tartar, salt and baking soda. Add flour mixture to sugar mixture; mix well.

Roll dough into balls; flatten with the bottom of glass dipped in sugar. Bake on cookie sheets in preheated oven at 350 degrees F for 10 minutes or until light brown.

Yield: 2 dozen cookies.

Carrot Cookies

Just don't tell the kids and they will never know that these yummy cookies contain a vegetable!

3/4 cup granulated sugar
3/4 cup butter or margarine, softened
1 egg
1 cup cooked and mashed baby carrots
2 teaspoons baking powder
2 cups all-purpose flour
1 teaspoon vanilla
1 tablespoon orange juice
1/2 teaspoon salt
Grated rind of 1 orange

Combine all ingredients. Drop by teaspoonfuls on greased cookie sheets. Bake in preheated oven at 350 degrees F until tops of cookies are light brown. When cool, frost with Orange Frosting.

Orange Frosting:

2 tablespoons butter, softened
2 1/2 tablespoons orange juice
2 cups confectioners' sugar to thicken

Mix butter and orange juice together. Add confectioner's sugar until reaching desired spreading consistency. Mix until smooth.

Yield: 2 dozen cookies.

Turtle Waffle Cookies

This recipe uses a waffle iron to "bake" the cookies.

1 1/2 cups granulated sugar
1 cup butter or margarine, softened
4 eggs
1/2 cup cocoa
2 cups all-purpose flour
1 teaspoon vanilla

Mix granulated sugar, butter or margarine, eggs, cocoa, flour and vanilla together with electric mixer. Preheat waffle iron. Spray waffle iron with non-stick cooking spray. Spoon 1 teaspoon on hot grill (one teaspoon on each square if using a 4 square). Cook 1 to 2 minutes. Frost when cool.

Chocolate turtle frosting:

6 tablespoons butter or margarine
6 tablespoons milk
1 1/2 cups granulated sugar
1/2 cup chocolate chips

Cook butter or margarine, milk and granulated sugar to rolling boil. Boil 1 minute. Remove from heat and add chocolate chips. Mix well and spread on cookies.

Yield: 2 dozen cookies.

Fork Cookies

This recipe may be varied by adding nuts, raisins, coconut or chocolate chips.

1 cup brown sugar, packed
1 cup white granulated sugar
1/2 cup vegetable oil
1/2 cup butter or margarine, softened
1 teaspoon vanilla
3 eggs
3 1/2 cups all-purpose flour
1/2 teaspoon salt
2 teaspoons baking soda
2 teaspoons cream of tartar

Mix brown sugar, granulated sugar, vegetable oil, butter or margarine, vanilla and eggs thoroughly. In a separate bowl, combine flour, salt, baking soda and cream of tartar; chill dough in refrigerator for 2 hours. Roll dough into 1-inch balls and place on cookie sheets.. Make a crisscross pattern with a fork on each cookie and bake in preheated oven at 350 degrees F for 10 to 12 minutes or until lightly browned.

Yield: 6 dozen.

Sweet Potato Cookies

Optionally add 1/2 cup of nuts to these yummy cookies.

1/2 cup butter, softened
1 cup brown sugar, packed
1 cup sweet potatoes, cooked and mashed
2 eggs, beaten
1 teaspoon vanilla
2 1/2 cups all-purpose flour
1 teaspoon salt
2 teaspoons baking powder
1/2 teaspoon ground allspice
1/2 teaspoon baking soda
1/2 cup milk

In a large bowl, cream butter and brown sugar together. Add sweet potatoes, eggs and vanilla; mix well. In separate bowl, mix flour, salt, baking powder, allspice and baking soda. Add flour mixture to sugar mixture. Add milk; mix well. Drop rounded teaspoonfuls of dough on greased or parchment-lined cookie sheets. Bake in preheated oven at 350 degrees F for 12 to 15 minutes.

Yield: 4 dozen.

One Hundred Cookies

This recipe is great when you need a lot of cookies, like for a bake sale.

1 cup granulated sugar
1 cup brown sugar, packed
1 cup butter or margarine, softened
1 teaspoon vanilla
1 cup vegetable oil
1 egg
3 1/2 cups all-purpose flour
1 teaspoon baking soda
1 teaspoon cream of tartar
1 cup crispy rice cereal (as Rice Krispies)
1 cup coconut
1 cup quick oats
1 cup nuts, chopped

Mix granulated sugar, brown sugar, margarine or butter, vanilla and oil together. Add egg. In a separate bowl, combine flour, baking soda and cream of tartar. Combine flour mixture and sugar mixture. Stir in rice cereal, coconut, oats and nuts. Form dough into 1-inch balls. Place on a cookie sheet and flatten with fork dipped in cold water. Bake in preheated oven for 10 to 15 minutes in 350 degrees F oven or until lightly brown.

Yield: 100 cookies.

Frosted Drop Cookies

These flavorful cookies are sweetened even more with icing.

1/2 cup margarine, softened
1 1/2 cups brown sugar, packed
1 teaspoon vanilla
2 eggs
2 1/2 cups all-purpose flour
1 teaspoon baking soda
1/2 teaspoon baking powder
1/2 teaspoon salt
1 cup sour cream
1/2 cup walnuts, chopped

In a large bowl, cream margarine, brown sugar and vanilla. Beat in eggs. In another bowl, combine flour, baking soda, baking powder and salt; add alternately with sour cream to sugar mixture. Stir in nuts. Drop by teaspoonful on greased cookie sheets. Bake in preheated oven at 350 degrees F for 10 to 12 minutes. Frost with Butter Icing.

Butter Icing
4 tablespoons butter
2 cups confectioners' sugar
1 teaspoon vanilla

Heat and stir butter in saucepan over low heat till golden brown. Remove from heat. Beat in confectioners' sugar and vanilla. Add enough hot water until of spreading consistency.

Yield: 4 dozen cookies.

Other Books by Victoria Steele:

101 Quick & Easy Chicken Recipes

101 Quick & Easy Cupcake and Muffin Recipes

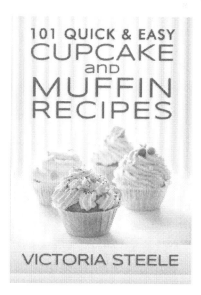

Available in Paperback and Kindle versions at Amazon.com

Made in the USA
Las Vegas, NV
07 November 2021